Daughter Zion

Joseph Cardinal Ratzinger

Daughter Zion

Meditations on the Church's Marian Belief

Translated by John M. McDermott, S.J.

Ignatius Press   *San Francisco*

Title of the German original:
Die Tochter Zion
© 1977 Johannes Verlag, Einsiedeln

Cover by Victoria Hoke Lane

With ecclesiastical approval
© 1983 Ignatius Press, San Francisco
All rights reserved
ISBN 978-0-89870-026-8 (PB)
ISBN 978-1-68149-129-5 (eBook)
Library of Congress catalogue number 82-084579
Printed in the United States of America

Contents

Preface

This small book, which I am now offering to the public, reproduces three lectures presented in the spring of 1975 in Puchberg bei Linz. After the Marian element had played a reduced role in the life of the Church for many years, people wanted, in all sobriety, to hear what actually now remained of Marian belief, and what should continue to remain. I therefore limited myself to providing an introduction which did not need to be complete with regard to details, but which did have to indicate correctly the perspective from which detail and whole alike might be properly understood.

Thus the intention and the limits of this publication are marked off at a single stroke. In my revision of it, I deliberately avoided changing its overall character. This book is intended, certainly not to replace a comprehensive treatise, but merely to open the reader's eyes to the layer of meaning that can then make the approach to larger works possible. To prevent the blurring of this small essay's limitations, I have intentionally left unaltered the more informal, improvisational characteristics which may mark the literary style of a lecture. Even an appropriate completion of the lectures' content, e.g., by a study of Matthew's testimony about the virgin birth, did not seem to me to be required by the overall objective of the work. I hope that this small book can, in its own way, help towards a new understanding and appropriation of what should not be lost in the Church's Marian belief.

Finally, I do not wish to neglect giving my heartfelt thanks to my respected friend Hans Urs von Balthasar for having patiently wrested this manuscript from me and for having, once again, seen it through the press after my call to become archbishop of Munich and Freising, which, announced publicly on the Feast of the Annunciation, overwhelmed me with new tasks.

Pentling, the Feast of the Ascension, 1977
Joseph Ratzinger

Chapter I

The Place of Mariology in the Bible

A discriminating observer of the Church's life today will discover a peculiar dichotomy in the Church's Marian belief and devotion. On the one hand, the impression is given that Mariology is a scaled-down duplicate of Christology that somehow arose on irrational grounds; or even more, it appears to be but the echo of ancient models found in the history of religions, which ineradicably returns to claim its position and value even in Christianity, although closer examination shows that there are neither historical nor theological grounds to support it. Historical support is lacking because Mary obviously plays scarcely any role in Jesus' career; she appears, rather, under the sign of misunderstanding. Theological support is lacking because the Virgin-Mother has no place in the structure of the New Testament credo. Indeed, many find no embarrassment in identifying the non-Christian origin of Marian belief and devotion: from Egyptian myths, from the cult of the Great Mother, from Diana of Ephesus, who, entirely on her own, became "Mother of God"

(θεοτόκος) at the council convened in Ephesus. . . .
On the other hand, there are those who plead for
a magnanimity with regard to diverse types of
piety: without puritanical tendencies, we should
just leave the Romans their madonnas.[1] Behind
this generosity can be seen an attitude which becomes noticeably stronger as a result of the trend
toward the rationalization of Christianity: namely,
the longing for a response in the religious sphere
to the demands of emotion; and after that, the
longing for the image of woman as virgin and
mother to have a place in religion as well. Of

[1] Cf. for example H. Küng, *Christ sein* (Munich, 1974),
452: "Thus one should allow more freedom to poetic statements in the Catholic tradition . . . and especially to forms
of personal or national piety. . . ." On another page Küng says:
"It is conspicuous that Mary plays . . . no role at all in the
early Christian witnesses" (448). Küng's exceptionally coarse
reassumption of the old, liberal hypothesis about the
θεοτόκος is on the same lines. He speaks of "Cyril of Alexandria's magnificently designed manipulation of the Council
of Ephesus and his (!) definition of the Mother of God before
the arrival at the Council of the other party from Antioch"
(450). "Especially in the East the fifth century arrived at the
definition of Mary . . . as 'Mother of God': a new, post-
biblical title, securely attested for the first time in the previous
century, yet now, after Cyril's action, received enthusiastically
by the people in the city of the old 'Great Mother' (originally
the virgin goddess Artemis, Diana). . ." (450).

10

course, mere tolerance in the face of manifold customs will not suffice to justify Marian piety. If its basis is as negligible as might appear from the considerations just mentioned, then the continued cultivation of Marian piety would be nothing but a custom contrary to truth. Such customs either wither away because their root, the truth, has dried up, or they continue to proliferate contrary to conviction, and thus destroy the correlation between truth and life. They thereby lead to a poisoning of the intellectual-spiritual organism, the results of which are incalculable.

Thus there is need of deeper reflection. Before entering into an examination of individual texts, we must direct our attention to the whole picture, the question of structure. Only in this way can a meaningful arrangement of individual elements be obtained. Is there any place at all for something like Mariology in Holy Scripture, in the overall pattern of its faith and prayer? Methodologically, one can approach this question in one of two ways, backwards or forwards, so to speak: either one can read back from the New Testament into the Old or, conversely, feel one's way slowly from the Old Testament into the New. Ideally both ways should coincide, permeating one another, in order to produce the most exact image possible. If one begins by reading backwards or, more precisely, from the end to the beginning, it becomes obvious that the image of Mary in the New Testament is woven entirely of Old Testament threads. In this reading, two or even three major strands of tradition can be clearly distinguished which were used to express the mystery of Mary. First, the portrait of Mary includes the likeness of the great mothers of the Old Testament: Sarah and especially Hannah, the mother of Samuel. Second, into that portrait is woven the whole theology of daughter Zion, in which, above all, the prophets announced the mystery of election and covenant, the mystery of God's love for Israel. A third strand can perhaps be identified in the Gospel of John: the figure of Eve, the "woman" *par excellence*, is borrowed to interpret Mary.[2]

These first observations, which we shall have to pursue later, offer us a guide into the Old Testament; they indicate where those elements lie which are pregnant with the future. All conse-

[2] Cf. esp. F. M. Braun, *La mère des fidèles* (Tournai, 1954); K. Wennemer, "Die heilsgeschichtliche Stellung Marias in johanneischer Sicht" in *Die Heilsgeschichtliche Stellvertretung der Menschheit durch Maria*, C. Feckes (Paderborn, 1954), 42–78.

quent Marian piety and theology is fundamentally based upon the Old Testament's deeply anchored theology of woman, a theology indispensable to its entire structure. Contrary to a widespread prejudice, the figure of woman occupies an irreplaceable place in the overall texture of Old Testament faith and piety.[3] This fact is seldom taken into sufficient consideration. Consequently, a one-sided reading of the Old Testament can open no door for an understanding of the Marian element in the Church of the New Testament. Usually only one side is taken into consideration: the prophets conducted a relentless battle for the uniqueness of God against the temptation to polytheism, and as matters then stood this was a battle against the goddess of heaven, a battle against the fertility religion, which imagined God to be man and woman. In practice this was a resolute battle against the cultic representation of the divine woman in temple prostitution, a battle against a cult which celebrated fertility by imitating it in ritual fornication. From this point of view, idolatry is usually referred to in the literature of the

[3] A penetrating discussion of this position is to be found in the small but important book of Louis Bouyer, *Mystère et ministères de la femme* (Paris, 1976); in German: *Frau und Kirche* (Einsiedeln: Johannes Verlag, 1977); in English: *Woman in the Church* (San Francisco: Ignatius Press, 1979).

Old Testament as "fornication". The rejection of these representations apparently led to the result that Israel's cult is primarily an affair of men, since the women certainly stay in the outer court of the temple.[4]

From the above considerations, it has been concluded that women had no role at all in the faith of the Old Testament, and that there is and can be no theology of woman because the Old Testament's chief concern is precisely the opposite: to exclude woman from theo-logy, from the language of God. This would then mean that Mariology *de facto* could only be seen as the infiltration of a non-biblical model. Consistent with this view would be the contention that at the Council of Ephesus (431), which confirmed and defended Mary's title as "Mother of God", the previously rejected "Great Mother" of pagan piety had in reality secured a place for herself in the Church. This view's presuppositions about the Old Testament, however, are false. For even though the prophetic faith rejects the model of deities set in "syzygies", i.e., in pairs, and the cultic expression of this model in sacred prostitution, it gives to

[4] Louis Bouyer, *Frau und Kirche*, 17 f., beautifully shows, nevertheless, that in the Old Testament an important cultic and religious position belongs to woman.

14

woman, in its own way, an indispensable place in its own model of belief and life, corresponding to marriage on the human level.[5] One could even say that if the worldwide fertility cults provide the immediate theological basis for prostitution, the consequence of Israel's belief in God with respect to the relation of man and woman expresses itself as marriage. Here, marriage is the immediate "translation" of theology, the consequence of an image of God; here and only here does there exist in the true sense a theo-logy of marriage, just as in the fertility cults there exists a theology of prostitution.[6] This is admittedly obscured in the Old Testament by many compromises, but what Jesus maintains in Mark 10:1–12 and what Ephesians 5

[5] There is more detail given in my contribution, "Zur Theologie der Ehe", in *Theologie der Ehe*, Greeven et al. (Regensburg-Göttingen, 1969), 81–115.

[6] Especially instructive in this respect is the study of Indian religion, even if the great ideal of Bhakti (Love) in the context of the figure of Krishna is presented in the symbol, not of married love, but of adultery and free love; cf. J. Neuner, "Das Christus-Mysterium und die indische Lehre von den Avataras", in *Das Konzil von Chalkedon* III, A. Grillmeier and H. Bacht (Würzburg, 1954), 785–824, esp. 801, note 34. The development goes much further in Shaktism; interesting texts and interpretations on this question in P. Hacker, *Prahlada: Werden und Wandlungen einer Idealgestalt* II (Wiesbaden, 1960), esp. 220 ff.

then further explains theologically is entirely the consequence of Old Testament theology. Along with this consequence, the idea and reality of virginity also emerge. For virginity is most intimately connected to the theological foundation of marriage; it does not stand in opposition to marriage, but rather signifies its fruit and confirmation.

But let us attempt, at long last, to get down to details. By tracing back into the Old Testament those elements by means of which the New Testament theologically interprets the figure of Mary, we have already hit upon three strands of a theology of woman.

1. In the first place we have to mention the figure of Eve. She is depicted as the necessary opposite pole of man, Adam. His being without her would be "not good" (Gen 2:18). She comes, not from the earth, but from himself: in the "myth" or "legend" of the rib is expressed the most intimate reference of man and woman to each other. In that mutual reference the wholeness of humanity is first realized. The necessary condition for the creation of mankind, to be fulfilled in the oneness of man and woman, becomes apparent here, just as previously Genesis 1:27 had

portrayed mankind from the very beginning as masculine and feminine in its likeness to God, and had mysteriously, cryptically, linked its likeness to God with the mutual reference of the sexes to each other. Admittedly the text also allows the ambivalence of this reference to become evident: woman can become a temptation for man, but simultaneously she is the mother of all life, whence she receives her name. In my opinion it is significant that her name is bestowed in Genesis 3:20 *after* the fall, *after* God's words of judgment. In this way the undestroyed dignity and majesty of woman are expressed. She preserves the mystery of life, the power opposed to death; for death is like the power of nothingness, the antithesis of Yahweh, who is the creator of life and the God of the living. She, who offers the fruit which leads to death, whose task manifests a mysterious kinship with death, is nonetheless from now on the keeper of the seal of life and the antithesis of death. The woman, who bears the key of life, thus touches directly the mystery of being, the living God, from whom in the last analysis all life originates and who, for that reason, is called "life", the "living one".[7] We shall see how precisely these

[7] Cf. the articles by Kapelrud and Ringgren in *Theologisches Wörterbuch zum Alten Testament* II, Botterweck and Ringgren, 794–789 and 874–898.

relationships are taken up again in the dogma of the Assumption.

2. In the Old Testament's history of promises, it is true that the patriarchs stand in the foreground as the true bearers of that history. Yet the mothers also played a specific role. In the history of the patriarchs, Sarah-Hagar, Rachel-Leah, and Hannah-Penina are those pairs of women in whom the extraordinary element in the path of the promises stands out. In each case the fertile and the infertile stand opposite each other, and in the process a re-markable reversal in values is reached.[8] In archaic modes of thought, fertility is a blessing, infertility is a curse. Yet here all is reversed: the infertile one ultimately turns out to be the truly blessed, while the fertile one recedes into the ordinary or even has to struggle against the curse of repudiation, of being unloved. The theological implication of this overthrow of values becomes clear only gradually; from it Paul developed his theology of spiritual birth: the true son of Abraham is not the one who traces his physical origin to him, but the one who,

[8] Parallel to this is the reversal of values in men, where the younger seems finally to be preferred to the elder; cf. my article "Fraternité", in *Dictionnaire de spiritualité* . . . V, 1141–1167.

in a new way beyond mere physical birth, has been conceived through the creative power of God's word of promise. Physical life as such is not really wealth; this promise, which endures beyond life, is what first makes life fully itself (cf. Rom 4; Gal 3:1–14; 4:21–31).

At an earlier stage of the Old Testament's evolution, a theology of grace was developed from this reversal of values in the song of Hannah, which is echoed in Mary's Magnificat: the Lord raises the humble from the dust, he lifts the poor from the ashes (1 Sam 2:8). God bends down to the humble, the powerless, the rejected, and in this condescension the love of God, which truly saves, shines forth both for Hannah and for Mary, in the remarkable phenomenon of unblessed-blessed women. The mystery of the last place (Lk 14:10), the exchange between the first and the last place (Mk 10:31), the reversal of values in the Sermon on the Mount, the reversal of earthly values founded upon *hybris*, all of this is intimated. Here also the theology of virginity finds its first, still hidden formulation: earthly infertility becomes true fertility. . . .

3. Near the end of the Old Testament canon, in its late writings, a new and, again, entirely original type of theology of woman is developed.

The great salvific figures of Esther and Judith appear, taking up again the most ancient tradition as it was embodied, for example, in the figure of the judge Deborah. Both women have an essential characteristic in common with the great mothers: one is a widow, the other is a harem-wife at the Persian court, and thus both find themselves—in different ways—in an oppressed state. Both embody the defeated Israel: Israel who has become a widow and wastes away in sorrow, Israel who has been abducted and dishonored among the nations, enslaved within their arbitrary desires. Yet both personify at the same time Israel's unconquered spiritual strength, which cannot boast as do the worldly powers and for that very reason knows how to scorn and overcome the mighty. The woman as savior, the embodiment of Israel's hope, thereby takes her place alongside the unblessed-blessed mothers. It is significant that the woman always figures in Israel's thought and belief, not as a priestess, but as prophetess and judge-savior. What is specifically hers, the place assigned to her, emerges from this.[9] The essence of what has previously been seen is repeated and strengthened: the infertile one, the powerless one becomes the savior because it is there that the

[9] Cf. Louis Bouyer, *Frau und Kirche*, 14 f.

locus for the revelation of God's power is found. After every fall into sin, the woman remains "mother of life".

4. In the theological short-story type of the woman-savior, one finds already presupposed and newly expressed what the prophetic preaching had developed with theological profundity from the image of the great maternal women and what is considered to be the proper center of the Old Testament's theology of woman: Israel herself, the chosen people, is interpreted simultaneously as woman, virgin, beloved, wife and mother. The great women of Israel represent what this people itself is. The history of these women becomes the theology of God's people and, at the same time, the theology of the covenant. By making the category of covenant comprehensible and by giving it meaning and spiritual orientation, the figure of the woman enters into the most intimate reaches of Old Testament piety, of the Old Testament relationship with God. Probably the notion of covenant was at first largely patterned after the model of ancient Eastern vassal indentures, in which the sovereign king assigns rights and duties. [10] This political and legal notion

[10] Cf. V. Hamp, "Bund", in *Lexikon für Theologie und*

of the covenant, however, is continually deepened
and surpassed in the theology of the prophets: the
covenant relation of Yahweh to Israel is a covenant
of marital love, which—as in Hosea's magnificent
vision—moves and stirs Yahweh himself to his
heart. He has loved the young maiden Israel with a
love that has proved to be indestructible, eternal.
He can be angry with the wife of his youth on
account of her adultery. He can punish her, but all
this is simultaneously directed against himself and
pains him, the lover, whose "bowels churn". He
cannot repudiate her without rendering judgment
against himself. It is on this, on his personal, innermost bewilderment as lover, that the covenant's
eternal and irrevocable character is based. "How
could I betray you, Ephraim, or hand you over,
Israel. . . ? My heart turns against me, my mercy
catches fire all at once. I do not act according to the
fire of my anger, I no longer annihilate Ephraim,
for I am God and not man, the Holy One in your
midst. I do not come to destroy all in flames" (Hos
11:8 f).[11] God's divinity is no longer revealed in his

Kirche II, 770–774; N. Lohfink, "Bund", *Bibellexikon*, ed. H.
Haag, 2nd ed. (Einsiedeln, 1968), 267–273.

[11] Cf. H. Gross, "Das Hohelied der Liebe Gottes: Zur
Theologie von Hosea 11", *Mysterium der Gnade* (Festschrift J.

ability to punish but in the indestructibility and constancy of his love.

This means that the relationship between God and Israel includes not only God but also Israel as woman, who in this relationship with God is at once virgin and mother. For this reason the covenant, which forms the very basis of the existence of Israel as a nation and the existence of each individual as Israelite, is expressed interpersonally in the fidelity of the marriage covenant and in no other way. Marriage is the form of the mutual relationship between husband and wife that results from the covenant, the fundamental human relationship upon which all human history is based. It bears a theology within itself, and indeed it is possible and intelligible only theologically. But above all, this also means that to God, the One, is joined, not a goddess, but, as in his historical revelation, the chosen creature, Israel, the daughter Zion, the woman. To leave woman out of the whole of theology would be to deny creation and election (salvation history) and thereby to nullify revelation. In the women of Israel, the mothers and the saviors, in their fruitful infer-

Auer), eds. H. Rossmann and J. Ratzinger (Regensburg, 1975), 83–91.

tility is expressed most purely and most profoundly what creation is and what election is, what "Israel" is as God's people. And because election and revelation are one, what ultimately becomes apparent in this for the first time is who and what God is.

Of course this line of development in the Old Testament remains just as incomplete and open as all the other lines of the Old Testament. It acquires its definitive meaning for the first time in the New Testament: in the woman who is herself described as the true holy remnant, as the authentic daughter Zion, and who is thereby the mother of the savior, yes, the mother of God. In passing, one might mention that the acceptance of the Canticle of Canticles into the canon of Scripture would have been impossible if this theology of love and woman had not existed. The Canticle is certainly, on technical grounds, a collection of profane love songs with a heavily erotic coloring. But once the songs have entered the canon, they serve as an expression of God's dialogue with Israel, and to that extent such an interpretation of them is anything but mere allegory.[12]

[12] Cf. Louis Bouyer, *Frau und Kirche*, 34 ff.; Henri de Lubac, *Der geistige Sinn der Schrift* (Einsiedeln: Johannes Verlag, 1956), 103.

5. In the last layers of the Old Testament, a further, remarkable line of development comes to light, which likewise does not lend itself to interpretation within the context of the Old Testament alone. The figure of wisdom (Sophia) attains central significance. She was probably taken over from Egyptian prototypes and then adapted to Israel's belief. "Wisdom" appears as the mediatrix of creation and salvation history, as God's first creature in whom both the pure, primordial form of his creative will and the pure *answer*, which he discovers, find their expression; indeed, one can say that precisely this concept of the answer is formative for the Old Testament idea of wisdom. Creation answers, and the answer is as close to God as a playmate, as a lover.[13]

We have previously noted that in order to interpret Mary, the New Testament refers back to the mothers of the Old Testament, to the theology of the daughter Zion, and probably also to Eve, and then ties these three lines of development together. We must now add that the Church's liturgy expands this Old Testament theology of woman insofar as it interprets the woman-saviors, Esther and Judith, in terms of Mary and refers the Wisdom texts to

[13] Gerhard von Rad, *Weisheit in Israel* (Neukirchen-Vluyn, 1970), esp. 189–228.

25

Mary. This has been sharply criticized by this century's liturgical movement in view of its christo-centric theology; it has been argued that these texts can and should allow only a christological interpretation. After years of wholehearted agreement with this latter view, it is ever clearer to me that it actually misjudges what is most characteristic in those Wisdom texts. While it is correct to observe that Christology assimilated essential elements of the wisdom idea, so that one must speak of a christological strand in the New Testament's continuation of the notion of wisdom, a remainder, nevertheless, resists total integration into Christology. In both Hebrew and Greek, "wisdom" is a feminine noun, and this is no empty grammatical phenomenon in antiquity's vivid awareness of language. "Sophia", a feminine noun, stands on that side of reality which is represented by the woman, by what is purely and simply feminine. It signifies the answer which emerges from the divine call of creation and election. It expresses precisely this: that there is a pure answer and that God's love finds its irrevocable dwelling place within it. In order to deal with the full complexity of the facts of the case, one must certainly consider that the word for "Spirit" in Hebrew (not, however, in Greek) is feminine. In that respect, because of the teaching about the Spirit, one can as it were practically have a presentiment of the primordial type of the feminine, in a mysterious, veiled manner, within God himself. Nevertheless, the doctrine of the Spirit and the doctrine of wisdom represent separate strands of tradition. From the viewpoint of the New Testament, wisdom refers, on one side, to the Son as the Word, in whom God creates, but on the other side to the creature, to the true Israel, who is personified in the humble maid whose whole existence is marked by the attitude of *Fiat mihi secundum verbum tuum*. Sophia refers to the Logos, the Word who establishes wisdom, and also to the womanly answer which receives wisdom and brings it to fruition. The eradication of the Marian interpretation of sophiology ultimately leaves out an entire dimension of the biblical and Christian mystery.

Thus we can now say the figure of the woman is indispensable for the structure of biblical faith. She expresses the reality of creation as well as the fruitfulness of grace. The abstract outlines for the hope that God will turn toward his people receive, in the New Testament, a concrete, personal name in the figure of Jesus Christ. At that same moment, the figure of the woman, until then seen only typologically in Israel although provisionally personified by the great women of Israel, also emerges with a name: Mary. She emerges as the personal epitome of the feminine principle in such a way that the principle is true only in the person, but the person as an individual always points beyond herself to the all-embracing reality, which she bears and represents.[14] To deny or reject the feminine aspect in belief, or, more concretely, the Marian aspect, leads finally to the negation of creation and the invalidation of grace. It leads to a picture of God's omnipotence that reduces the creature to a mere masquerade and that also completely fails to understand the God of the Bible, who is characterized as being the creator and the God of the covenant—the God for whom the beloved's punishment and rejection themselves become the passion of love, the cross. Not without reason did the Church Fathers interpret the passion and cross as marriage, as that suffering

[14] Hans Urs von Balthasar persuasively points to personalization as constitutive of the New Testament's figure of the covenant in "Umkehr im Neuen Testament", *Internationale katholische Zeitschrift* 3 (1974), 481–491; the Church's personal concreteness in Mary is one of the fundamental concerns of his thought; cf. most recently *Der antirömische Affekt* (Freiburg: Verlag Herder, 1974), 153–187.

in which God takes upon himself the pain of the faithless wife in order to draw her to himself irrevocably in eternal love.[15]

[15] Cf. the profound theology of the *sacrum commercium* in the late work of E. Przywara. There he first gave to his *analogia entis* doctrine its full theological form (theology of the cross), which has been unfortunately hardly noticed. See esp. *Alter und Neuer Bund* (Vienna, 1956).

Chapter II

The Marian Belief of the Church

So far we have dealt directly only with statements of the Old Testament, yet in such a way that we read them "backwards", from the viewpoint of the New Testament; we considered the Old Testament as present in the New. That was deliberate. The whole New Testament is rooted in the Old and wants simply to be a rereading of the Old Testament in light of what occurred with and through Jesus of Nazareth.[1] Nonetheless, in a certain respect Mariology ties the knot joining Old and New. Mariology cannot be found apart from its union with the prophetic theology of the bridal people of God. From the beginning, in Luke and John, the Marian authors of the New Testament, Mariology is woven entirely out of the Old Testament's faith. If Christ brings the marked distinction and break from the Old Testament, in the novelty of his word, his life, his

[1] Cf. the classical expression of this view in the Emmaus pericope (Lk 24:13–35); J. Wanke, *Die Emmauserzählung* (Leipzig, 1973); also a very fine treatment is L. Stöger, *Das Evangelium nach Lukas* II (Düsseldorf, 1966), 313–325.

passion, his cross, and his resurrection, Mary, through her silence and faith, incarnates the continuity realized in the poor of Israel, in those to whom is addressed the beatitude: Blessed are the poor "in *pneuma*". In essence the beatitudes only offer variations of the Magnificat's spiritual center: He ejects the mighty from their throne, he elevates the humble. The center of the Magnificat contains simultaneously the center of the biblical theology of the people of God. This insight illuminates the distinctive structures of the Marian dogmas. For if such is the case, they *cannot* be deduced from individual texts of the New Testament; instead they express the broad perspective embracing the unity of both Testaments. They can become visible only to a mode of perception that accepts this unity, i.e., within a perspective which comprehends and makes its own the "typological" interpretation, the corresponding echoes of God's single history in the diversity of various external histories.

These methodological insights shed light on the reasons for the suspicion against Mariology that has arisen in modern times, either inducing a rebellion against Mariology or driving it into a dangerous romanticism. Wherever the unity of Old and New Testaments disintegrates, the place of a healthy Mariology is lost. Likewise this unity of the Testaments guarantees the integrity of the doctrines of creation and of grace. In modern times, however, the loss of typological exegesis (seeing the cohesion of the one history in the many histories) has actually led to the separation of the Testaments, and by isolating the doctrine of grace it has at the same time increasingly threatened the doctrine of creation. In this respect one can note in passing how Mariology serves as an indicator of the correct positioning of the christological accents.

This in no way means that the New Testament texts lose their importance. We are merely indicating the perspective within which they can develop their full significance. As we are here concerned not with a scientifically complete elaboration of Mariology but merely with a reflective explication of the substance of the Church's Marian piety, we can take a shorter path to our goal: this will not be a Mariology constructed piece by piece out of its New Testament components; instead, I shall propose immediately the three great Marian dogmas: their biblical foundations will emerge almost spontaneously to the reflective spirit. What, then, are these affirmations?

1. The oldest, basic Marian dogma of the Church maintains that Mary is Virgin (ἀεὶ παρθένος: Sym-

bola, DS 10–30; 42/64; 72; 150) and Mother; indeed, she may be called "Mother of God" (θεοτόκος: DS 251, Council of Ephesus). Both are closely related: when she is called Mother of God, this title primarily expresses the unity of divinity and humanity in Christ, which is so intimate that one cannot, for the sake of the corporeal events such as birth, construct a merely human Christ, cut off from the entirety of his person. That was the argument of the Nestorians who would only permit the designation "Mother of Christ" (Χριστοτόκος) instead of the title "Mother of God". Yet such a division of the figure of Christ, aseptically separating the biological-human from the divine existence, conceals anthropological and theological decisions of immense import: behind the formula "Mother of God" stands the conviction that the unity of Christ is so profound that the merely corporeal Christ can nowhere be distilled out of it, because in man the corporeal is also the human-corporeal, as modern biology confirms.[2] Furthermore, in this man the human is human in a unique way, i.e., as the humanity of the God-man. The divine united itself so really and truly to man that no threshold of the human hinders it, but it penetrates

[2] See esp. the works of A. Portmann, and most recently the summation of the entire path of his research: *An den Grenzen des Wissens* (Vienna-Düsseldorf, 1974), esp. 81–107.

this very human being in his entirety; consequently it penetrates his body too. Then birth is not to be reduced to a merely somatic act, as it often seems to be in our philosophy of 'emancipation'; ultimately this philosophy is profoundly hostile to both the body and creation since it considers the sexual constituent of man as a small and irritating detail having nothing to do with man as such. If, however, the unity of man is to be understood in accordance with the faith of the councils, Mary's maternity is most intimately involved with the mystery of the Incarnation as such and reaches into the very heart of the mystery. Thus the christological affirmation of God's Incarnation in Christ becomes necessarily a Marian affirmation, as *de facto* it was from the beginning. Conversely: only when it touches Mary and becomes Mariology is Christology itself as radical as the faith of the Church requires. The appearance of a truly Marian awareness serves as the touchstone indicating whether or not the christological substance is fully present. Nestorianism involves the fabrication of a Christology from which the nativity and the Mother are removed, a Christology without mariological consequences. Precisely this operation, which surgically removes God so far from man that nativity and maternity—all of corporeality—remain in a different sphere, indicated unambiguously to the Christian consciousness that the discussion no longer concerned In*carn*ation (becoming *flesh*), that the center of Christ's mystery was endangered, if not already destroyed. Thus in Mariology Christology was defended. Far from belittling Christology, it signifies the comprehensive triumph of a confession of faith in Christ which has achieved authenticity.

The believing Church, following the witness of Matthew and Luke, saw that the specific characteristic of maternity, which engages the entire human being for the sake of the one to be born, was realized in the unity of Mother and Virgin, vindicating the abiding Old Testament image of her who is blessed and not blessed, fruitful and barren. Being unwed and infertile was previously the curse of those abandoned, without a future and, therefore, without a true present. Now, as virginity, this state can forever validly represent the mystery of renunciation and fruitfulness and, together with marriage to which it refers, express the special characteristic of the God who, in creation and redemption, seeks out and blesses man.

2. From the same root of the theology of the people of God and its fulfillment in Mary's maternity there slowly grows the certitude of Mary's

sinlessness as the expression of her special election: *Immaculata conceptio* (DS 2800–2804).

3. The confession of Mary's sinlessness engenders in turn the conviction of her participation in the destiny of her Son, the resurrection, and in his conquest of death (DS 3900–3904).

1. The Primary Marian Dogma: Virgin and Mother

a. The New Testament texts

The purification of Christianity, the search for its original essence, is carried on today, in the era of historical consciousness, almost entirely by seeking its oldest forms and establishing them as normative. The original is confused with the primitive. By contrast the faith of the Church sees in these beginnings something living, that conforms to its own constitution only insofar as it *develops*.

What path led to the confession of Mary's virginal motherhood? Here again, we are not pursuing a strictly scientific analysis. We simply wish to gain an overview of the principal stages in the growth of the relevant tradition. In Paul's writings the question of Jesus' nativity does not yet play a theological role; his faith develops wholly from the confession of the cross and resurrection. Only in one passage can we ascertain a remote prelude to those affirmations which later will be handed on explicitly in the infancy narratives of Matthew and Luke. When in Galatians 4:4 Paul says of Jesus that he is "born of woman" he is simply concerned to show that Jesus participated in the complete ordinariness of being human, that he entered fully into the

human condition.[3] For Paul this means princi-
pally that Jesus submitted himself to the burden
of the Law, of a religion that had become law
and as a result created more anxiety and division
than hope and unification. With us he carried our
burden and our ordinariness. More is not to be
found in this text. Of course, when the entire
context is considered and its thought is, as it
were, extrapolated toward future development,
one can perhaps, in a modest way, already catch
the faint cadences of the future theology of the
Christmas mystery. For within the whole context
of this passage Paul establishes a relation between
Christian existence and Abraham's two sons, Isaac
and Ishmael. He affirms that the heir of the promise is not just the one who traces his lineage to
Abraham according to the flesh (Ishmael), but
the one to whom the Spirit, the living power of
the promise, bore testimony. He inserts the Christian, who is in Jesus, into this lineage of spiritual
birth, into the lineage of Isaac, that expression of

[3] Cf. on this text H. Schlier, *Der Brief an die Galater*
(Göttingen, 1962), 194 ff.; F. Mussner, *Der Galaterbrief* (Freiburg, 1974), 268 ff. Strangely, M. Dibelius, the resolute
opponent of the historical character of the virgin birth tradition, tries to find evidence in Galatians 4 for St. Paul's
acquaintance with what he postulated to be a hellenistic virgin
birth theologoumenon; indeed, Paul and Philo are all the
evidence there is for the existence of the "theologoumenon".
Neither of them stands the test; cf. footnote 4.

the new birth from Abraham which believers in Christ enjoy (4:21–31).[4]

That is nothing more than a prelude; the lines of thought are not developed. This occurs for the first time in the writings of Matthew and Luke, and in a twofold manner. First, our attention must be turned to the special function of the genealogical tables which delineate Jesus' ancestry while simultaneously attempting an interpretation of his nature. Matthew's genealogy presents Jesus as a son of Abraham, yet primarily it characterizes him as the true David, who fulfills the sign of hope which David had become for his people. Luke proceeds further; he follows Jesus' path back to Adam, "who came from God" (3:38). Adam is purely and simply "man", the human being. The genealogy extending back to Adam not only indicates that in Jesus Israel's royal hope is fulfilled; it also answers the question about human nature, which in the course of its wanderings and gropings is searching for itself. Jesus is the man for

---

[4] Cf. Schlier, ibid., 207–228; Mussner, ibid., 316–334. For the discussion of the above thesis of Dibelius ("Jung-frauensohn und Krippenkind", in *Botschaft und Geschichte* I [Tübingen, 1953], 1–78, esp. 28) see E. Nellessen, *Das Kind und seine Mutter* (Stuttgart, 1969), 97–109; O. Michel and O. Betz, "Von Gott gezeugt", in *Judentum, Urchristentum, Kirche* (Festschrift J. Jeremias) (Berlin, 1960), 18.

all men, the man in whom man's divine destination, his divine origin, finds its goal. In him man's fragmented nature is unified and preserved in unity with the God from whom it derives and whom, in its forlorn state, it seeks.

Both genealogies are concerned with the historical and human context of Jesus' life. Nevertheless, both are convinced that Jesus can be the maturing fruit of history only because in him a new power has entered into the withered tree of history—because he is not only "from below". He is certainly the fruit of this tree, but the tree can only bear fruit because it is rendered fertile from without. Jesus' origin is from below, yet simultaneously from above—and this is no contradiction. He is entirely man precisely because he does not have his origin only in this earth. Matthew points this out insofar as the pattern of his genealogy, which joins one member to another through the phrase "he begot", is broken in the final statement: Joseph, the husband of Mary, *from whom was born* Jesus, called the Christ (1:16). Luke makes the same point when Jesus does not figure as the son of Joseph, but is assigned his legitimate place in the series as the one who "was considered to be Joseph's son" (3:23).

The intimation of the mystery here in question is developed in greater detail by the infancy narratives (Mt 1:18–25; Lk 1–2). We need not enter

into all the details. We will briefly mention just
a few characteristics of the Lucan text which are
important for the entire understanding of the
figure of Mary. It is important first to note the
setting which Luke chooses for his deliberate contrast with the pre-history of John the Baptist. The
annunciation of John's birth occurs in the temple
to an officially functioning priest—according to
the prescribed, official disposition of the Law,
linked to its cult, its local setting, and its repre-
sentatives. The annunciation to Mary happens to
a woman, in an insignificant town in half-pagan
Galilee, known neither to Josephus nor the Tal-
mud. The entire scene was "unusual for Jewish
sensibilities. God reveals himself, where and to
whom he wishes."[5] Thus begins a new way, at
whose center stands no longer the temple, but the
simplicity of Jesus Christ. *He* is now the true
temple, the tent of meeting.

The salutation to Mary (Lk 1:28–32) is modelled
closely on Zephaniah 3:14–17: Mary is the daughter Zion addressed there, summoned to "rejoice",
informed that the Lord is coming to her. Her fear
is removed, since the Lord is in her midst to save

[5] H. Schürmann, *Das Lukasevangelium* I (Freiburg, 1969),
42; cf. also M.-J. Lagrange, *Das Evangelium von Jesus Christus*
(Heidelberg, 1949), 19.

her.[6] Laurentin makes the very beautiful remark on this text: ". . . As so often, the word of God proves to be a mustard seed. . . . One understands why Mary was so frightened by this message (Lk 1:29). Her fear comes not from lack of understanding nor from that small-hearted anxiety to which some would like to reduce it. It comes from the trepidation of that encounter with God, that immeasurable joy which can make the most hardened natures quake."[7] In the address of the angel, the underlying motif in the Lucan portrait of Mary surfaces: she is in person the true Zion, toward whom hopes have yearned throughout all the devastations of history. She is the true Israel in whom Old and New Covenant, Israel and Church, are indivisibly one. She is the "people of God" bearing fruit through God's gracious power.

Finally, we must pay attention to the terms in which the mystery of the new conception and birth is deliberately stated: The Holy Spirit will come upon you, and the power of the Most High will overshadow you. In the so-called *parallelismus membrorum* two images of the ineffable mystery from different strands of the tradition are here

[6] R. Laurentin, *Struktur und Theologie der lukanischen Kindheitsgeschichte* (Stuttgart, 1967), 75–82; idem, *Court traité de théologie mariale* (Paris, 1953), 25.

[7] Laurentin, *Court traité*, 25.

meshed. The first image alludes to the history of creation (Gen 1:2) and so characterizes the event as a new creation: the God who called being out of nothingness, whose Spirit hovered over the abyss, he who as "creator Spirit" is the ground of all beings—this God discloses new creation from within the old creation. In this way the radical incision which Christ's coming signifies is most emphatically marked; its novelty is of such an order that it penetrates to the ground of being and can derive from nowhere if not from the creative power of God himself. The second image—"the power of the Most High will overshadow you" —belongs to the theology of Israel's cult; it refers to the cloud which overshadows the temple and thereby indicates the presence of God. Mary appears as the sacred tent over whom God's hidden presence becomes effective.

Before we turn to a concluding theological evaluation, we still have to answer two questions. The first concerns the origin of the tradition elaborated by Matthew and Luke. Modern exegesis shows how both evangelists re-formed the basic material in view of their own theological insights and purposes; this "literary" share of the evangelists in the formation of the tradition is certainly not to be minimized. Exegesis also shows, of course, that both evangelists employ the material of a tradition already at hand, previously formed by the community passing it on. Regarding Luke, Schürmann believes that he can identify as the previous link in the tradition's chain a Judaean community between 60 and 70 A.D.[8] It cannot be doubted that Luke himself wished to refer to Mary (and thereby presumably to the wider circle of Jesus' blood relations) (2:19, 51). The reception of these passages into the gospel is accordingly a special event in the history of the tradition: it means that a previously private tradition, preserved in a limited circle, is taken up into the Church's public proclamation and receives the dignity of a public tradition of the entire Church. This seems to me an important insight for the often raised question of the age of these traditions. What distinguishes the Easter tradition from the Christmas tradition is not simply age as such; Luke traces the nativity stories back to Mary's memory and there is no reason to mistrust him in regard to the tradition's core, which is already theologically formed, especially since the "brothers of the Lord", a group hardly to be ignored for its position and influence, appear as the transmitting community. Concerning the traditional core, therefore, the difference consists not in age, but in the different status which each tradition at first acquired and in

[8] Schürmann, *Das Lukasevangelium* I, 145.

the relatively late date at which, in a particular stage of the Christian confession's inner development, it became meaningful and necessary to integrate these traditions into the common, public confession of the Church. This does not occur until the inner locus is prepared for it and the temporal distance, which reverence required, is bridged.

The second remark concerns the continued efficacy of this affirmation within New Testament proclamation. Corresponding to Paul's "prelude" is a Johannine use of the theme that transforms what is historical and unique into what is spiritual and universal—thus, not a postlude, but rather the statement of a fugal theme that opens up ever new possibilities of modulation. In the prologue to his gospel John characterizes Christians as those "who are not born from blood nor the will of the flesh or of a man, but from God" (1:13). Here the Pauline motif is connected to the Matthean-Lucan tradition to constitute a new unity: to become a Christian means to enter into the mystery of the new birth of Jesus Christ, by one's rebirth to participate in his birth. Naturally even on this point we cannot avoid the disputed question about the approach of the fourth gospel. As in his sacramentology (baptism, eucharist) and eschatology (resurrection now and on the last day), did not John want to transcend the "vulgar-catholic" understanding by elevating it into the spiritual and existential realm? Has he not been 're-attached' to a view he really wanted to transcend? Within the limits of our reflections we need not discuss this question any further. Yet in view of all the data one thing seems clear to me: the full weight of the fourth gospel's spiritual teaching is grounded in the conviction that it has a foundation in reality. The "existential" would say nothing more if it were the interpretation of nothing. Christian rebirth is possible because it really occurred in Jesus and therefore became a possibility for us all.

b. The theological meaning

These remarks have already brought us into the question of interpretation. Why was that fact handed on, i.e., accepted into the public, communal tradition of the Church? Only by seeking the theological ground for this step can we see clearly the importance which was and is attributed to the fact of Mary's virginity in her maternity. What is the issue here? The two principal points seem to be the following:

1. It involves a declaration about God's action with respect to man, and thereby a declaration about man himself. Jesus' conception and birth signify a new involvement in history that exceeds the uniqueness belonging to every single human

47

being. At this point God himself begins anew. What begins here has the quality of a new creation, owing to God's own totally specific intervention. Here is the true "Adam", who again, and in a more profound sense than previously, comes "from God" (cf. Lk 3:38). Such a birth can only happen to the 'barren' woman. What was promised in Isaiah 54:1 has become for Luke a concrete reality in the mystery of Mary. Israel, powerless, rejected by men, barren, has brought forth fruit. In Jesus God initiated a new beginning in the midst of a barren and hopeless humanity. This beginning is not the result of mankind's own history, but a gift from above. A new Incarnation starts with Jesus. In contradistinction to all the elect before him, he not only *receives* the Spirit, but also he *is* in his earthly existence through the Spirit, and therefore he is the fulfillment of all the prophets: the true Prophet. In this way Mary, the barren, blessed one, becomes a sign of grace, the sign of what is truly fruitful and salvific: the ready openness which submits itself to God's will.

2. It involves also, however, a primary, authentic christological declaration, which H. Schürmann describes as follows:

> Because the child in his origin is a work of God, he will be thoroughly 'holy'. The Holy Spirit will not imbue him, like John, 'from his mother's womb' (1:15), but God's Pneuma will endue him

with concrete existence in a creative bestowal of
life, and, determining his innermost being, make
it 'holy'.[9]

The very contrast with John, who, like Jeremiah,
in receiving his vocation in his mother's womb
(1:4), incarnates the Old Testament's man of God,
shows Luke's intention clearly: here is more than a
prophet, here is a "Son", because his being as such
is the fruit of the Spirit.

3. Hans Urs von Balthasar has plumbed this
connection using the logic of being human and
the logic of the Incarnation, a process we already
met in our consideration of the title "Mother of
God". If the Son is truly incarnate this event really
reaches into the "flesh" and, inversely, because
man is one and entire, the "flesh" reaches into the
personal center of the Logos. Despite the indestructible distinction of natures between God and
man, Incarnation means a concrete unity of life. In
Jesus' being as man this unity so realizes itself that
his whole human life enters into the filial exchange
of the Son with the Father, thinking and existing
from the Father and to the Father. Let us listen to
the words of Hans Urs von Balthasar:

> Could this man, who stood in such a unique
> relation to the "Father in heaven", to whom in
> every respect he was indebted, to whom he totally

[9] Ibid., 53 f.

entrusted himself, to whom he entirely returned himself, could this man simultaneously owe his existence to another father? To put it bluntly, could he have two fathers, which would humanly have caused him to be indebted to two fathers? For he did not live in our so-called "fatherless society" in which the fourth commandment has apparently paled into total disappearance and in which the relation between children and parents no longer rests on a humanly unified relation of concerned, reverential, deferential love, but is reduced to a fortuitous sexual act which places on the child no essential obligation to his parents. . . . Must not Jesus' exclusive relationship to his heavenly father have offended deeply the carpenter Joseph, if he had been his natural parent? And could Jesus, who had intensified the necessity of keeping the Ten Commandments (Mk 10:19), himself have transgressed this commandment which is so vital for all cultures?[10]

To be born without an earthly father has an inner necessity for him who alone might say to God 'my Father', who was Son from the depth of his being as man, Son of this Father. Joseph's genealogy, which both gospels present, points to the legal

[10] Hans Urs von Balthasar, "Empfangen durch den Heiligen Geist, geboren von der Jungfrau Maria", in *Ich glaube: Vierzehn Betrachtungen zum Apostolischen Glaubensbekenntnis*, ed. W. Sandfuchs (Würzburg, 1975), 39–49; citation from 42.

position of Jesus in the society of his day, points to
David and, therefore, to the messianic dignity.
The virginal birth, however, points to the Sonship, points to the Father, and thereby points to
what was for Jesus infinitely more essential than
the Messianic dignity, which he valued very little
—at least as it was currently interpreted by his
contemporaries in *their* exegesis of the Old Testament. The virgin birth is the necessary origin of
him who is the Son and who as Son first endows
the messianic hope with a permanent significance
extending far beyond Israel.[11] In this "new birth"

[11] With this statement I would like to emphasize clearly the
limits of my frequently cited observation in *Einführung in das
Christentum* (Munich, 1968), 225, that Jesus' divine sonship
would not of itself exclude an origin in a normal marriage. I
wanted only to emphasize very clearly the distinction of
biological and ontological levels of thought and to clarify that
the ontological statements of Nicaea and Chalcedon are not as
such identical with the statements about the virgin birth. This
should not be used to deny that, despite the distinction of
levels, a deep, even an indissoluble correspondence exists
between the two levels, between Jesus' unity of person with
the eternal Son of the eternal Father and the earthly fatherless-
ness of the man Jesus. Yet I admit that I did not make the
point clearly enough; to that degree von Balthasar's critique,
ibid., 43, is justified. But to everyone who reads not only
the cited passage of my book (225) but also the whole section
(222–230) it must otherwise be crystal clear that the use
of my remarks in R. Pesch, *Das Markusevangelium* I (Freiburg,
1976), 323, contradicts my meaning.

(the Roman liturgy says *nova nativitas*), which simultaneously included the abandonment of earthly fertility, of self-disposal, and of the autonomous planning of one's own life, Mary as Mother is truly "the bearer of God"; she is more than the organ of a fortuitous corporeal event. To bear the "Son" includes the surrender of oneself into barrenness. Now it becomes clear why barrenness is the condition of fruitfulness—the mystery of the Old Testament mothers becomes transparent in Mary. It receives its meaning in Christian virginity beginning with Mary.

Nevertheless it is well known that the fact of the virgin birth, its actual historicity, is sharply contested and abandoned even by many Catholic theologians. It is said that the spiritual meaning, not the biological fact, can alone be of importance for theology, and the biological is to be considered only a symbolic means of expression. But however plausible this exit appears, it only leads to a dead end. Closer scrutiny reveals the illusion. The cavalier divorce of "biology" and theology omits precisely man from consideration; it becomes a self-contradiction insofar as the initial, essential point of the whole matter lies precisely in the affirmation that in all that concerns man the biological is also human and especially in what concerns the divinely-human *nothing* is "merely biological". Banishment of the corporeal, or sexual, into pure biology, all the talk about the "merely biological", is consequently the exact antithesis of what faith intends. For faith tells us of the spirituality of the biological as well as the corporeality of the spiritual and divine. On this point the choice is between all or nothing. The attempt to preserve a spiritual, distilled remainder after the biological element has been alienated denies the very spiritual reality which is the principal concern of the faith in the God become flesh.

Whence do the difficulties truly derive? I think that two levels must be distinguished. The first level is the one of obvious problems appearing on center stage, including the undoubtedly serious questions of the historical evidence; nevertheless it is of only secondary importance. Usually only these problems are mentioned; as a result the debate remains a battle of shadows, because the real reasons—on the second level—do not come into play. We must therefore try to uncover them.

Let us begin, nonetheless, with a glance at the usual objections—the reasons of secondary importance, as I prefer to call them. We have already met one of these objections during our consideration of the New Testament texts: we are warned that we are dealing with a relatively late tradition. Yet epistemologically this contributes little to the discussion, for antiquity as such provides no standard of truth. It can be objected that, however true this is regarding the intellectual development of insights, in a case of statements about *events* temporal proximity to the event reported is a decisive criterion. In reply a distinction must be stressed in the analysis of the phrase "relatively late". The literary form may be relatively late, but the tradition given in that form had already existed in another form; no historical critique can exclude the possibility that the simple nucleus of the account is significantly more ancient. Furthermore, the agreement with regard to the nucleus of the account from two mutually independent traditions which otherwise show considerable formal diversities in detail is a norm of some significance—and this is what we can ascertain through a study of the sources of Matthew and Luke. In addition, the heavily Jewish-Christian accent of the entire account carried great weight, and it points surely to those circles which alone could be originators of such statements. Finally, we have already concluded that there are very good reasons in favor of the later reception into the public tradition of what had first been privately transmitted. What is "late" is the public reception, not the nucleus of the tradition itself.

The second group of the more obvious objections refers to the alleged derivation of the idea of the virgin mother from parallels in the history of religions. Ever since Martin Dibelius, the reference to Philo of Alexandria (c. 13 B.C.–45/50 A.D.) has been a favorite; on the basis of Philo's exegesis of the maternity of the great women of the Old Testament (Sarah, Leah, Rebecca, Zipporah) Dibelius wanted to show that the idea of the exclusive agency of God in certain births was a *theologoumenon* of hellenistic Judaism, which the Christians then applied to Jesus' begetting.[12] Carrying further Dibelius' initial suggestion G. Guthknecht attempted to show that it was not a genuinely hellenistic notion, but "an ancient Egyptian *theologoumenon*".[13] In response E. Nellessen demonstrated with irrefutable accuracy that Dibelius' interpretation of Philo's texts is based on amazingly sloppy scholarship.[14] Anyone

[12] Dibelius, "Jungfrauensohn und Krippenkind", cf. footnotes 3 and 4.

[13] G. Guthknecht, *Das Motiv der Jungfrauengeburt in religionsgeschichtlicher Beleuchtung* (Greifswald, 1952), 83.

[14] Nellessen, *Das Kind und seine Mutter*, 104–107.

55

reading the text for himself without having previously capitulated to the authority of the great
scholar can discover that what Philo offers is an
allegorical and moralistic interpretation of the patriarchs, not a "hellenistic *theologoumenon*" about
the parthenogenesis of men of God. The most
that can be gathered from Dibelius for our interests
is that these texts serve as a spiritual harbinger for
the understanding of virginity, as well as for its
special manner of fruitfulness and closeness to God.
To that extent he prepares a spiritual climate in
which the message of the Christmas mystery
could be interpreted. But these texts are not a
model of the historical event itself. Guthknecht's
attempt to move everything back to Egyptian
sources has likewise failed; for the individual details
Nellessen's work may be referred to.[15] G. Delling
has persuasively proven that all further parallels
from the history of religion, however painstak-
ingly assembled from various sources, miss the
mark.[16] In the proper sense of the word there are
no parallels from religious history to the Christmas
stories of the New Testament. There are only
motifs which touch on the Christian assertion
more or less closely. I see nothing negative in this:

[15] Ibid., 108 f.
[16] "παρθένος", *Theologisches Wörterbuch zum Neuen Testament* V, 824–835.

these may be the expression of a psychological archetype in whose confused longing, as in all authentic archetypes, a deep knowledge of reality is expressed. Be the reality ever so remote, the human heart with its intimations and anticipatory questions already awaits its fulfillment.

The confidence with which Jesus' birth from the virgin is denied today cannot be explained on the basis of the historical problems. The underlying, actual cause which spurs the historical questioning lies elsewhere: in the difference between our modern world-view and the biblical affirmation and in the presupposition that this biblical affirmation can find no place in a world scientifically explained. At this point then the question must be raised: what *is* a "world-view"? To what extent is it a determinant of our knowledge? Closer scrutiny and reflection—perhaps against the background of Bultmann's utilization of the modern world-view—of components of our own and previous world-views allows us to say this: a world-view is always a synthesis of knowledge and values, which together propose to us a total vision of the real, a vision whose evidence and power of persuasion rest upon the fusion of knowledge and value. This is, however, the very basis of the problem: the plausible values embedded in the practice of a specific time attain through their conjunction with what is known a certitude that they do not enjoy of themselves and which, under certain circumstances, can become a barrier to more exact knowledge. The plausible can direct investigation toward truth, but it can also be truth's opponent.[17]

The world-view which would force us psychologically to declare the virginal birth an impossibility clearly does not result from knowledge, but from an evaluation. Today, just as much as yesterday, a virgin birth is improbable, but in no way purely impossible. There is no proof for its impossibility, and no serious natural scientist would ever assert that there was. What 'compels' us here to declare the maximum inner-worldly *improbability* an *impossibility*, not only for the world but also for God, is not knowledge but a structure of evaluations with two principal components: one consists in our tacit cartesianism—in that philosophy of emancipation hostile to creation which would repress both body and birth from the human

[17] Cf. A. Görres, "Glaube und Unglaube in psychoanalytischer Sicht", in *Internationale katholischer Zeitschrift* 2 (1973), 481–504; also the references in P. Berger, *A Rumour of Angels* (Garden City, 1969).

reality by declaring them merely biological;[18] the other consists in a concept of God and the world that considers it inappropriate that God should be involved with *bios* and matter. In reality, precisely when we talk about corporeality and raise suspicions about the soul, we are dualists.

Let us pause here in order to summarize what we have seen and to attempt the subsequent steps. Now we can say that the real reason behind the reasons against the confession of Mary's virginity lies not in the field of a historical (exegetical) knowledge, but in the presuppositions of a worldview. The exegetical arguments explicate this presupposition with the instruments of historical thought without, however, being compellingly vindicated by it. This first insight yields a further one: the cause of the denial is due to the worldview, yet its consequences touch our understanding of God (our God-view). Contrary to the usual presentation the real dispute occurs not between historical naiveté and historical criticism, but between two preconceptions of God's relationship

[18] I have attempted to present a clearer picture of the dualistic character of the radical philosophies of emancipation in my little book *Der Gott Jesu Christi* (Munich, 1976), 26 ff. and 34 ff.

to his world. For the preconception that what is most improbable in the world is also impossible for God conceals the tacit presupposition that it is impossible both for God to reach into earthly history and for earthly history to reach him. His field of influence will be limited to the realm of the spirit. And with this we have landed back in pagan philosophy such as Aristotle elaborated with a singular logic; prayer and every relation to God is, in his view, "cultivation of the self". If in the final analysis this is reality, nothing but the "cultivation of the self" can remain.[19]

Having examined these presuppositions and consequences, it is clear that we are concerned not with peripheral details, but with the central questions: Who was Jesus? Who or what is man? Then, finally, with the greatest question of all: Who or what is God? From this last question man's fate ultimately depends—even in an atheistic vision of man the question of God is decisive, negatively, for the question of man. In the framework of the New Testament's faith the testimony to Jesus' birth from the Virgin Mary is not an idyllic nook of devotion, a tiny, private chapel of the two evangelists, an optional extra. The question of

[19] Cf. *Nichomachean Ethics* X, 9, etc.; F. Dirlmeier, *Nikomachische Ethik* (Darmstadt, 1956), 597 ff.

God is at stake: Is God a depth of being somewhere which, as it were, nourishes the deep roots of all things in some unimaginable way, or is he the one who acts with power, who knows and loves his creation, is present to it and effectively works in it from first to last, even today? The alternatives are simple: does God act or not? Can he act at all? If not, is he really "God"? What does the word "God" mean anyway? Faith in God, who has *remained* the creator in the new creation —*Creator Spiritus*—is at the center of the New Testament and is its primary motive force. The affirmation of Jesus' birth from the Virgin Mary intends to affirm these two truths: (1) God really acts—*realiter*, not just *interpretative*, and (2) the earth produces its fruit—precisely *because* he acts. The *Natus ex Maria virgine* is in its nucleus a strictly theo-logical affirmation that bears witness to the God who has not let creation slip out of his hands. On this are based the hope, the freedom, the assurance, and the responsibility of the Christian.

2. Freedom from Adam's Sin

We now consider the two objections raised against the dogma of the Immaculate Conception. The first objection maintains that preservation from original sin is a fact (if it is at all). Facts, however, cannot be deduced through speculation, but can be known only through some communication (revelation). But such a communication regarding Mary does not exist. The first Christian millennium knows nothing of this fact. Consequently the assertion of her Immaculate Conception transgresses the proper boundaries of speculation. The second objection holds that such a declaration about Mary puts in question the universality of grace. Medieval theology disputed this question, and the theology of the Reformation reformulated the problem more fundamentally and sharply when it defined grace essentially as the justification of a *sinner*. It should be sufficient on this point to refer to Karl Barth, probably the most impressive representative of Protestant belief in our century. In any theology wishing to attribute to Mary some type of independent role in salvation history he discerns the attempt to "illuminate" and ground the miracle of revelation "a posteriori, from man's viewpoint, from man's receptivity".[20]

[20] Karl Barth, *Kirchliche Dogmatik* I, 2, 158 f.; cf. also the important essay by B. Langemeyer, "Konziliare Mariologie und biblische Typologie: Zum ökumenischen Gespräch

Therefore the acceptance of Mary means in his eyes that she, "despite the sins of which . . . she is guilty . . . is accepted as the conceiver of the eternal God himself."[21] On this point Barth stands in the line of Luther's strict opposition of law and gospel: between God and man there is no correspondence (analogy), only contradiction (dialectic). Where God's activity is delineated from the viewpoint of correspondence, pure grace, the unmerited justification of the sinner, is called into question.

But is this so? The Franciscan B. Langemeyer, following the Second Vatican Council, pointed emphatically to the typology ("doctrine of correspondence") binding Old and New Testaments in an interior unity of promise and fulfillment.[22] As a form of interpretation typology includes analogy, similarity in dissimilarity, unity in diversity. Our reflections so far have rested on this insight, on the affirmation of the most profound unity of the Testaments. They are now illustrated in a concrete case. Langemeyer draws our attention to the fact that the prophets' preaching of judgment (containing the moment of discontinuity) is accompanied by the reference to Israel's

über Maria nach dem Konzil", *Catholica* 21 (1967), 295–316, esp. 306.

[21] Barth, I, 2, 214; Langemeyer, 315, note 61.

[22] Langemeyer, ibid.

holy remnant that will be saved—a thought that St. Paul expressly takes up in Romans 11:6, seeing it fulfilled in the Christian Israel. "Holy remnant" means that continuity does not rest in God's will alone while destruction and contradiction occupy the field of history, but that there is continuity *in* history too: God's word is not spoken in vain.

> It would have been absurd to talk about a surviving remnant, a holy root, if the Old Covenant had led to apostasy and sin. In that case there would only be a new beginning.[23]
>
> . . . The activity of God does not strike purely vertically into a history that had come about through his prior activity. Faith does not fall from heaven. It is conceived through the witness of faith in a horizontal-historical encounter.[24]
>
> . . . In Mary the corporeal offspring of the chosen people coincides perfectly with the faith in the promise given to this people. As a result, it was not by human accomplishment, but by the grace of the covenant that holds sway in history, that the salvific significance due the Old Testament according to God's plan finally attained its fulfillment, namely, the conceiving in body and spirit of the eschatological kingdom of God which he willed Israel to mediate to the peoples of the earth.[25]

[23] Ibid., 304.
[24] Ibid., 313. [25] Ibid., 314.

To repeat, the holy remnant signifies that God's word really brings forth fruit, that God is not the only actor in history, as if history were only his monologue, but that he finds a response that is *truly* a response. As the holy remnant Mary signifies that in herself Old and New Covenants are really one. She is entirely a Jewess, a child of Israel, of the Old Covenant, and as such a child of the full covenant, entirely a Christian: Mother of the Word. She is the New Covenant in the Old Covenant; she is the New Covenant *as* the Old Covenant, *as* Israel: thus no one can comprehend her mission or her person if the unity of the Old and New Testaments collapses. Because she is entirely response, correspondence [*Entsprechung*], she cannot be understood where grace seems to be opposition and response, the real response of the creature, appears to be a denial of grace; for a word that never arrived, a grace that remained solely at God's disposal without becoming a response to him would be no grace at all, but just a futile game. The essence of woman was already defined in Eve: to be the complement that exists entirely in its derivation from the other, and nevertheless remains its complement. Here this essence reaches its acme: pure derivation from God and at the same time the most complete creaturely complement—a creature that has become response.

Having said this, the first question admittedly remains unanswered: Well and good, replies our objector, in the realm of thought this may be a meaningful assertion, but how are we justified in affirming that Mary is this "holy remnant"? Is not this to conjure a fact from a principle? In reply one must observe that the concept "fact" cannot be applied, in its positivistic severity at any rate, to original sin. For original sin itself is not a fact in a positivistic sense, observable like the fact that Goethe was born on August 28, 1749. Original sin is a "fact", a reality, of a different type, known only through typology; the basic text, Romans 5, is a typological interpretation of the Old Testament. Original sin became recognizable in the type Adam, and in his recurrence at the turning points of history. Its affirmation rests upon the typological identification of every single man with man as such, with average man, with man from the beginning on. Original sin was not handed on in the tradition (and previously communicated) from the beginning as a fact. It has been identified in a theological (reflex) manner through typological Scriptural exegesis. To have missed this truth was perhaps the principal error of the neoscholastic doctrine on original sin. The moment this error was introduced, in whatever degree, in conjunction with the total lack of understanding of typological identification, it led to the questioning of original sin, the impossibility of thinking or talking about it. This being so, it is also clear that freedom from original sin cannot be communicated as a fact; it is only to be recognized by theology, and in no other way.

One need not search very far for a typological identification grounding Mary's freedom from original sin. The Epistle to the Ephesians describes the new Israel, the bride, as "holy", "immaculate", "luminously beautiful", "without spot, wrinkle, or the like" (5:27). Patristic theology further developed this image of the *Ecclesia immaculata* in passages of lyrical beauty.[26] Consequently, from the very beginning there is a doctrine about the *Immaculata* in Scripture and especially in the Fathers, even if it concerns the *Ecclesia immaculata*. Here the doctrine of the *Immaculata*, like the whole of later Mariology, is first anticipated as ecclesiology. The image of the Church, virgin and mother, is *secondarily* transferred to Mary, not vice versa. So if the dogma of the Immaculate Conception transferred to the concrete figure of Mary those assertions which primarily belong to the antithesis new-old Israel, and are in this sense a typologically developed ecclesiology, this means that Mary is presented as the beginning and the personal concreteness of the

[26] Cf. Hugo Rahner, *Maria und die Kirche* (Innsbruck, 1951); A. Müller, *Ecclesia-Maria*, 2nd ed. (Fribourg, 1955).

Church. It entails the conviction that the rebirth of the old Israel into the new Israel, of which the Epistle to the Ephesians spoke, achieves in Mary its concrete accomplishment. It proclaims that this new Israel (which is simultaneously the true old Israel, the holy remnant preserved by the grace of God) is not only an idea, but a person. God does not act with abstractions or concepts; the *type*, of which the ecclesiology of the New Testament and the Fathers speak, exists as a *person*. At this point another question may be raised: very well, the New Testament does contain a doctrine of the *Immaculata*; all those Marian assertions are not new as such, but only by their personification in terms of Mary. But how can we justify the personification of the type at this point and nowhere else? The answer is not difficult. For the typological identification of Mary and Israel, the presence of the type in the person, is clearly present in Luke's writings—and, in a different way, in John's.[27] It is no less part of the framework of biblical theology than the systematic interpretation of the Adam-Christ type is part of the doctrine of original sin. Through the Lucan equation of the true daughter Zion with the listening-believing Virgin it is fully present, in essentials, in the New Testament.

[27] Cf. R. Laurentin, *Court traité de théologie mariale* (Paris, 1953); see also Hans Urs von Balthasar, "Wer ist die Kirche?", in *Sponsa Verbi* (Einsiedeln: Johannes Verlag, 1961), 148–202.

There remains a final question: What does the expression "preserved from original sin" actually mean? Karl Rahner correctly noted that the point at issue here cannot be a chronological one (Mary is justified earlier than others). Such a transferral of justification back into the very act of coming into existence, such an identification of birth and rebirth, of life and grace, must have an axiological meaning transcending temporal anticipation.[28] To that extent the question arises here of the very meaning of original sin; indeed, perhaps it is only by introducing this second typological strand that we can resolve the muddle produced by considering exclusively the Adam-strand of interpretation. Only on this basis, perhaps, can we move towards a meaningful solution. The affirmation of Mary's freedom from original sin prunes away every naturalistic perspective. Thus we may say that original sin is not an assertion about a natural deficiency in or concerning man, but a statement about a relationship that can be meaningfully formulated only in the context of the God-man relation. The essence of sin can only be understood in an anthropology of relation, not by looking at an isolated human being. Such an anthropology is even more essential in the case of grace. We could therefore describe original sin

[28] Karl Rahner, "Die unbefleckte Empfängnis", in *Schriften zur Theologie* I (Einsiedeln, 1954), 223–237.

as a statement about God's evaluation of man; evaluation not as something external, but as a revealing of the very depths of his interior being. It is the collapse of what man is, both in his origin from God and in himself, the contradiction between the will of the Creator and man's empirical being.

This contradiction between God's "is" and man's "is not" is lacking in the case of Mary, and consequently God's judgment about her is pure "Yes", just as she herself stands before him as a pure "Yes". This correspondence of God's "Yes" with Mary's being as "Yes" is the freedom from original sin. Preservation from original sin, therefore, signifies no exceptional proficiency, no exceptional achievement; on the contrary, it signifies that Mary reserves no area of being, life, and will for herself as a private possession: instead, precisely in the total dispossession of self, in giving herself to God, she comes to the true possession of self. Grace as dispossession becomes response as appropriation. Thus from another viewpoint the mystery of barren fruitfulness, the paradox of the barren mother, the mystery of virginity, becomes intelligible once more: dispossession as belonging, as the locus of new life.

Thus the doctrine of the *Immaculata* reflects ultimately faith's certitude that there really is a holy Church—as a person and in a person. In this sense it expresses the Church's certitude of salvation.[29] Included therein is the knowledge that God's covenant in Israel did not fail but produced a shoot out of which emerged the blossom, the Savior. The doctrine of the *Immaculata* testifies accordingly that God's grace was powerful enough to awaken a response, that grace and freedom, grace and being oneself, renunciation and fulfillment are only apparent contradictories; in reality one conditions the other and grants it its very existence.

[29] To this extent the concretization of the doctrine of grace, presupposed in the statement of the *conceptio immaculata*, is closely connected with Luther's central problem, even if it appears in a very different perspective.

3. The Bodily Assumption into Heavenly Glory

Here we face the even more insistent objection that the raising of Mary is a fact that must be witnessed and communicated, not just invented. This was behind the emphatic protest of German theology before the official proclamation of the dogma, most insistently in the famous series of articles by B. Altaner, whose entire historical erudition demonstrated that, as far as sources are concerned, there is no witness to such a doctrine before the sixth century.[30] So it is clear that the point at issue cannot be historical tradition of an historical fact; the affirmation is misunderstood if it is considered or presented as such. This makes it decisively different from Jesus' resurrection. Doubtless his resurrection also transcends history and in this sense offers us no historical fact of the usual type, but it is essential for the resurrection that it reach into temporal existence and announce itself in an historical account. The text of the Bull of 1950 did justice to this distinction insofar as it does not speak of Mary's *resurrectio* (*anastasis*), but of her *assumptio ad coelestem gloriam*—not of "resurrection", but of the "assumption" of the body

[30] B. Altaner, "Zur Frage der Definibilität der Assumptio B. M. V.", *Theologische Revue* 44 (1948), 129–140; cf. M. Schmaus, *Katholische Dogmatik* V, "Mariologie" (Munich, 1955), 232 ff.

and soul into heavenly glory. In this way it clearly defines the content of the article of faith as a theological, not an historical, affirmation.

What then does this mean? To clarify the matter, one would have to pay attention to the dogma's historical development and the factors in its formulation. This would show that the decisive driving force behind the declaration was veneration for Mary, that the dogma, so to speak, owes its origin, impetus, and goal more to an act of homage than to its content.[31] This also becomes clear in the text of the dogmatic proclamation, where it is said that the dogma was promulgated for the honor of the Son, for the glorification of the mother, and for the joy of the entire Church.[32] This dogma was intended to be an act of veneration, the highest form of Marian praise. What the orient achieves in the form of liturgy, hymns, and rites, took place in the occident through the form of a dogmatic proclamation, which was intended to be, so to speak, a most solemn form of hymnology. This is how it should be understood. It distinguishes the last two Marian dogmas in a certain respect from the earlier form of ecclesial confessions, even though the doxological element always played a more or less accentuated role.

[31] More detail can be found in R. Laurentin, *La question mariale* (Paris, 1963).

[32] *Denzinger-Schönmetzer*, 3903.

We can therefore say that the dogmatic proclamation of 1950 was an act of Marian veneration in the form of a dogmatic statement, which, by exalting the Mother to the highest degree, was intended to be a liturgy of faith. The declaration's content is entirely oriented to veneration, yet the veneration inversely makes use of this content as its foundation: the veneration refers to one who is alive, who is at home, who has actually arrived at her goal on the other side of death. We can also say that the formula of the assumption makes explicit what veneration presupposes. Every veneration involves the predicate *Sanctus* (*Sancta*) and has as its presupposition life with the Lord; it only has meaning if the object of veneration is alive and has attained the goal. To that extent one could say that the dogma of the Assumption is simply the highest degree of canonization, in which the predicate "saint" is recognized in the most strict sense, i.e., being wholly and undividedly in eschatological fulfillment. Here we see the fundamental biblical context which supports the whole declaration. In noting that the article about the Assumption only paraphrases what is presupposed by the highest degree of veneration, in the very same breath we must remember that the gospel itself prophesies and requires veneration for Mary: "Behold, from henceforth all generations will call me blessed" (Lk 1:48)—this is a commission to the Church. In recording it, Luke presupposes that there was already praise of Mary in the Church of his time and that he considers it a commission of the Church for all generations. He saw its inception in Elizabeth's greeting: "Blessed are you who have believed . . ." (Lk 1:45).[33]

This earliest form of Marian devotion once more reflects the unity of the Testaments which is characteristic of the whole Marian theme: The God of Israel is named by men to whom he has manifested his greatness and in whose lives he becomes visible and present. They are as it were his *name* in history, through them he himself possesses names, and through and in them he becomes more accessible. He is called the God of Abraham, Isaac and Jacob. To name him includes naming the patriarchs, just as, inversely, to name the patriarchs means thinking of him and recognizing him. Not to name the men in whom he himself became visible is the same as ingratitude; it is amnesia and it is characteristic of Israel's faith that it has and is memory. Thus Marian praise harmonizes with that picture of God which associates the patriarchs with the name of God and recognizes the extolling of God in the extolling of the patriarchs. Once this is established we cannot exclude from our treatment the interpretation of the

[33] Cf. F. Mussner, "Lk 1,48 f; 11,27 f und die Anfänge der Marienverehrung in der Urkirche", *Catholica* 21 (1967), 287–294.

God of the patriarchs which Jesus expounded in Mark 12:18-27. Here he places the theme of the God of the patriarchs in the context of the resurrection theme, joining both themes in such a way that they mutually condition each other. He proves the resurrection not from individual texts of later prophetic or apocalyptic literature (which would in any case not have been persuasive in a discussion with the Sadducees), but from the notion of God: God, who allows himself to be called the God of Abraham, Isaac and Jacob, is not a God of the dead, but of the living. The resurrection itself proves that these names belong to the name of God: "As for the dead, that they will rise, have you not read in the book of Moses, in the section on the thorn bush, how God said to him, 'I am the God of Abraham, the God of Isaac, and the God of Jacob'? Yet God is not a God of the dead but of the living—you have erred" (12:26 f.). The right to veneration includes the certitude of the conquest of death, the certitude of the resurrection.[34]

Again, of course, we meet with an objection. Conquest of death, yes, but why put it in the highest form, in the ultimate-eschatological, as the formula *corpore et anima* intimates (which one is tempted to translate simply as "eschatological")?

[34] I treated these connections in greater detail in my essay "Taufe, Glaube und Zugehörigkeit zur Kirche", in *Internationale katholische Zeitschrift* 5 (1976), 218–234.

A very straightforward answer can be offered: This is permitted because this name—Mary— stands for the Church itself, for *its* definitive state of salvation. However, before we explore this answer, we shall do well to discuss another intermediary notion which plays a significant role in the text of the dogmatic proclamation.

The way human life is, implanted in a world where death is the condition of life, birth is always ambivalent, simultaneously a dying and a becoming. The words of judgment in Genesis 3:16 describe exactly this fate of man, and the ambiguity of the figure of Eve expresses the ambiguity of biological becoming: birth is part of death, it happens under the sign of death and points to the death that it in a certain sense anticipates, prepares, and also presupposes.[35] To give birth to life always signifies at the same time to open oneself to death. Now, if Mary is really the one giving birth

[35] The religions of the world frequently express this in a profound way. Important references to this are found in the still unpublished dissertation written at Regensburg by B. Adoukonou, *Jalons pour une théologie africaine: Essai d'une Herméneutique chrétienne du Vodoo dahoméen*. In the voodoo religion treated by Adoukonou (the form practiced in Dahomey, Benin) after a child's birth the placenta and umbilical cord are carried in solemn ceremony to the grave and buried in a circle symbolizing time; on top of it a tree, the symbol of life, is planted: this ritually shows the indivisible alliance of birth and dying, life and death, which stands at the center of this whole religion.

to God, if she bears him who is the death of death and is life in the full sense of the word, this being the Mother of God is really a "new birth" (*nova nativitas*): a new way of giving birth inserted into the old way, just as Mary is the New Covenant in the midst of the Old Covenant, even as a member of the Old Covenant. This birth is no dying, but only a becoming, a bursting forth of life that casts off dying and leaves it behind once and for all. The title "Mother of God" points, on the one hand, back to the Virgin: this life is not received through the every-day dying and becoming but is pure beginning. On the other hand, the title points to the Assumption: from this birth comes only life, no death. This new "generation" does not demand the surrender of the old self as its *sine qua non*, rather it effects the ultimate validation of the whole.

Here also we see the connection with the Immaculate Conception. It can perhaps be paraphrased like this: where the totality of grace is, there is the totality of salvation. Where grace no longer exists in the fractured state of *simul justus et peccator*, but in pure "Yes", death, sin's jailer, has no place. Naturally this involves the question: What does the assumption of body and soul into heavenly glory mean? What, after all, does "immortality" mean? And what does "death" mean? Man is not immortal by his own power, but only in and through another, preliminarily, tentatively, fragmentarily, in children, in fame, but finally and truly only in and from the Entirely-Other, God. We are mortal due to the usurped autarchy of a determination to remain within ourselves, which proves to be a deception. Death, the impossibility of giving oneself a foothold, the collapse of autarchy, is not merely a somatic but a human phenomenon of all-embracing profundity. Nevertheless, where the innate propensity to autarchy is totally lacking, where there is the pure self-dispossession of the one who does not rely upon himself (= grace), death is absent, even if the somatic end is present. Instead, the whole human being enters salvation, because as a whole, undiminished, he stands eternally in God's life-giving memory that preserves him as himself in his *own* life.[36]

So we return to what was previously suggested. We said that whoever may be glorified and praised together *with* God's name is alive. We added that in the case of Mary and in her case alone (as far as we know) it applies in a definitive, unconditional way, because she stands for the Church itself, for its definitive state of salvation, which is no longer a promise awaiting fulfillment but a fact. Here Colossians 3:3 seems to me to be significant: "You

[36] I have presented the problem of immortality and resurrection in detail in my eschatology, which will be brought out in the fall 1977 by Pustet as the ninth volume in the *Kleine katholische Dogmatik*, edited by J. Auer and myself.

have died, and your life is hidden with Christ in God." That is, there is something like an "ascension" of the baptized, of which Ephesians 2:6 explicitly speaks: "He raised you up with him and placed you in heaven at the right hand of Christ Jesus." According to that text Baptism is a participation in Jesus' ascension as well as his resurrection. The baptized person, as such and on that account, is already included in the ascension and lives his hidden (his most individual) life there, in the elevated Lord. The formula of the "assumption" of Mary's body and soul loses every trace of speculative arbitrariness in this perspective. The Assumption is actually only the highest form of canonization. She gave birth to the Lord "with her heart before her body" (Augustine), and therefore faith, i.e., the interior substance of Baptism according to Luke 1:45, can be predicated of her without restriction, realizing in her the very quintessence of Baptism. Thus it is said that, in her, death was swallowed up by Christ's victory and that, in her, everything still resisting Baptism (faith) has been conquered without remainder through the death of the earthly life. On the basis of the New Testament, through the integration of Luke 1:45 and Ephesians 2:6, this affirmation refers transparently to Mary, and it forms a bond with the typological contexts which we have been investigating: she who is wholly baptized, as the personal reality of the true Church, is at the same time not merely the Church's *promised* certitude of salvation but its *bodily* certitude also. The Church is already saved in her: the new Israel is no more to be rejected. It has already ascended into heaven. There are precious texts from the Church Fathers on this topic, which, nevertheless, only expand what has already been given in Scripture.[37]

One more remark in conclusion: Luke recounts in the story of Mary's visit to Elizabeth that when Mary's greeting rang out John "leaped for joy in his mother's womb" (1:44). To express that joy he employs the same word σκιρτᾶν (leap) that he used to express the joy of those to whom the beatitudes are addressed (Lk 6:23). This word also appears in one of the old Greek translations of the Old Testament to describe David's dance before the Ark of the Covenant after it had returned home (II Sam 6:16 Symmachus).[38] Perhaps Laurentin is not entirely off the mark when he finds

[37] Cf. Hugo Rahner, *Himmelfahrt der Kirche* (Freiburg, 1961); idem, *Mater Ecclesia: Lobpreis der Kirche aus dem ersten Jahrtausend christlicher Literatur* (Einsiedeln-Cologne, 1944); idem, *Maria und die Kirche* (Innsbruck, 1951); K. Delahaye, *Erneuerung der Seelsorgsformen aus der Sicht der frühen Patristik* (Freiburg, 1958).

[38] Cf. R. Laurentin, *Struktur und Theologie der lukanischen Kindheitsgeschichte* (Stuttgart, 1967), 91–94. Laurentin's proofs for the parallelism between Lk 1:39–44, 56 and II Sam 6:2–11 are not absolutely overwhelming, yet their weight seems to have been undervalued by Schürmann, *Das Lukasevangelium*, 64 f., note 161. Positive in Laurentin's sense are Stöger, *Das*

the whole scene of the visitation constructed as a parallel to the homecoming of the Ark of the Covenant; thus the leaping of the child continues David's ecstatic joy at the guarantee of God's nearness. Be that as it may, something is expressed here that has been almost entirely lost in our century and nonetheless belongs to the heart of faith; essential to it is the joy in the Word become man, the dance before the Ark of the Covenant, in self-forgetful happiness, by one who has recognized God's salvific nearness. Only against this background can Marian devotion be comprehended. Transcending all problems, Marian devotion is the rapture of joy over the true, indestructible Israel; it is a blissful entering into the joy of the Magnificat and thereby it is the praise of him to whom the daughter Zion owes her whole self and whom she bears, the true, incorruptible, indestructible Ark of the Covenant.[39]

Evangelium nach Lukas, 54 f., and Nellessen, *Das Kind und seine Mutter*, 108.

[39] To the whole theme of this book cf. esp. W. Beinert, *Heute von Maria reden* (Freiburg, 1974); A. Müller, *Du bist voll der Gnade* (Olten, 1957). For devotion to Mary cf. the translation of Paul VI's Apostolic Letter *Marialis Cultus* for which W. Beinert wrote an introduction: *Die rechte Pflege und Entfaltung der Marienverehrung* (Leutesdorf, 1974); W. Beinert, ed., *Maria heute ehren* (Freiburg, 1977). For the Mariology of the Second Vatican Council cf. R. Laurentin, *La Vierge au Concile* (Paris, 1965); G. Philips, *L'Eglise et son mystère au deuxième Concile du Vatican* II (Paris, 1968), 207–289, 322.